Designing
Everyday
Things

Designing Everyday Things

Integrated Projects for the Elementary Classroom

Helen Clayfield
Robyn Hyatt

HEINEMANN
Portsmouth, NH

HEINEMANN
A division of Reed Elsevier Inc.
361 Hanover Street
Portsmouth, NH 03801-3912
Offices and agents throughout the world

First published in 1993 by
Oxford University Press Australia
253 Normanby Road
South Melbourne
Victoria, Australia 3205

Library of Congress Cataloging-in-Publication Data

Clayfield, Helen.
    Designing everyday things : integrated projects for the elementary
classroom / Helen Clayfield, Robyn Hyatt.
        p.   cm.
    Originally published: Victoria, Australia: Oxford University
Press Australia, 1993.
    ISBN 0-435-08359-7 : $14.50
    1. Industrial arts—Study and teaching (Elementary) 2. Education,
Elementary—Activity programs. 3. Technology—Study and teaching
(Elementary) I. Hyatt, Robyn. II. Title.
LB 1594.C53 1994
372.3'58--dc20   94-8874
                                                    CIP

Cover illustrated by Christina Miesen
Printed in the United States of America on acid-free paper
99 98 97 96 95 94 EB 1 2 3 4 5 6 7 8 9

Contents

Design

Energy Source

Glossary

Foreword to U.S. Edition

Rosemary Williams

Integrated curriculum approaches are weaving their way into American schools, allowing for new and exciting combinations of topics and objectives. When these approaches are blended with open–ended, problem–solving, student–conscious values in teaching, real breakthroughs can occur!

For teachers interested in exploring the world of design, science, and technology with their students, *Designing Everyday Things* provides a wonderful springboard for experimentation. It offers all the opportunities for success and "whoops" experiences that adult designers enjoy.

As educators, we have tended to put technology on a distant pedestal. We feel uncomfortable in the worlds of engineering, product design, technical applications, and materials. But, as this book shows, these worlds can belong to all of us if we pay attention to the things we use every day, to the role of play in learning and working, and to our own values about technology.

On page 4, the authors define technology as "a problem-solving process based on satisfying a need in a practical way." Sometimes, however, when we begin to teach and learn about technology, we get so purposeful and goal-oriented that we forget to include the process of play, with its explorations, trials and errors, mishaps, wonderful surprises, and unexpected inventions and outcomes. One of the important contributions that Helen Clayfield and Robyn Hyatt have shared in this book is their commitment to the notion that we don't have to strive to become involved in the world of design and technology—each one of us already is an everyday technologist. And this includes our students, who are being technologists whether they are playing with toys, using a computer, or building a bird feeder.

I would like to share my own definition of technology, too, to address many aspects of the book that go beyond problem-solving processes. What works for me is to understand technology as a whole culture in its own right—"the culture of the material world." In this context, technology involves the same components as any culture—processes, myths, rituals, artifacts, people, and language.

The spirit and activities in this book promote a rich variety of experiences. The authors provide opportunities to dispel some myths (especially some gender myths), engage in conversations about our technical dreams and ideas and problems, develop an identity as an active participant in technology, explore the array of materials that surround us, and acknowledge a sense of technological style unique to each of us.

I encourage you to explore your own sense of technology, and to watch and listen carefully as your students reveal theirs as they work on the projects. Above all, enjoy designing and exploring and messing about with everyday things!

Introduction

In 1990 we had the opportunity to run a specialist technology program from P–6.

Co-operative group work, real purposes for literacy learning and equal opportunity issues formed a significant part of our own classroom programs and we saw technology as an ideal opportunity to expand these aspects into a new learning area.

The specialist program began as a team-teaching experience. In this way we could provide support and encouragement to each other while trialling something new. This approach proved to be very successful.

We set clear goals and objectives for the program, monitoring and assessing these as the year progressed. We were encouraged by the positive responses we received from students, parents and teachers.

Teachers from other schools visited and we gave in-services to our own staff and others. This book comes as a result of these teachers requesting activities and advice about starting technology in the classroom.

We believe the ideas contained in this book will be of value to teachers planning technology programs for the first time, and teachers more experienced in this area.

Robyn Hyatt
Helen Clayfield

Acknowledgements

The authors and publisher are grateful to the following for permission to use copyright material.

Ronda and David Armitage for the reproduction of the two-page spread from *The Lighthouse Keeper's Lunch* (Puffin Books, 1977); Sidchrome for the photographs of tools; Maurine Corridon for the photograph of the Leaning Tower of Pisa; NSW Tourism Commission for the photograph of the Sydney Harbour Bridge.

Disclaimer
Every effort has been made to contact and acknowledge copyright holders. Where the attempt has been unsuccessful the publisher would be pleased to hear from the copyright holders to rectify any omission.

Thanks to Rob, Don, Jennifer, Christopher, Andrew and Amanda.

Teacher's Information

Why Teach Technology?

Technology offers ideal opportunities for all students to be successful learners. This occurs because technology:
- is an effective and interesting way to teach all subject areas, for example, purposes for reading and writing, measuring, estimating, problem-solving, research, etc.
- provides a practical means of testing theories
- provides students with ideal situations for co-operative learning
- provides opportunities for students to explore a wide variety of materials such as textiles, ceramics, wood, plastics, etc.
- provides a supportive environment for students to take risks, make decisions, achieve success and enhance self-esteem
- provides open-ended problem-solving opportunities
- plays a vital role in the Equal Opportunity Program
- provides access to equipment and tools
- provides an insight into social, cultural and historical implications of technological change.

What is Technology?

Technology is a problem-solving process based on satisfying a need in a practical way. Think of everyday items around you and how they have been developed in response to needs.

For classroom purposes, technology provides students with an effective model to demonstrate learning as a process. Each stage of the process is as important as the final product.

Need

- Inventions occur as the result of a need.

Ideas

- Ideas are generated from the need.

Designing

- Students make decisions about:
  — materials
  — methods of construction
  — energy source
  — how they will work, for example in groups or individually.
- After these decisions have been made a plan is produced. This plan can take many forms depending on the students' age, background knowledge and the purpose of the task.

Making and Doing

- What materials are available? How will the materials be used?
- Students use materials and tools to produce a model which follows their plan.

Testing

- Does it work or does it need modification?
- Students check the success of their design and have the opportunity to make changes. Ways of testing the model will depend on the nature of the design brief.

Modifying

- Students should have the option to alter their design.
- The design may have been unsuccessful and need changing, or the student may see potential for improvement.

4

Recording and Reporting

- This is the final step in the process. Students should present information about their design, including:
  — design brief
  — materials and tools used
  — energy source
  — methods of construction
  — testing data
  — any necessary modifications.

Needs, Ideas, Designing, Making and Doing, and *Testing* are the components involved in the technology process. It is a cyclic process.

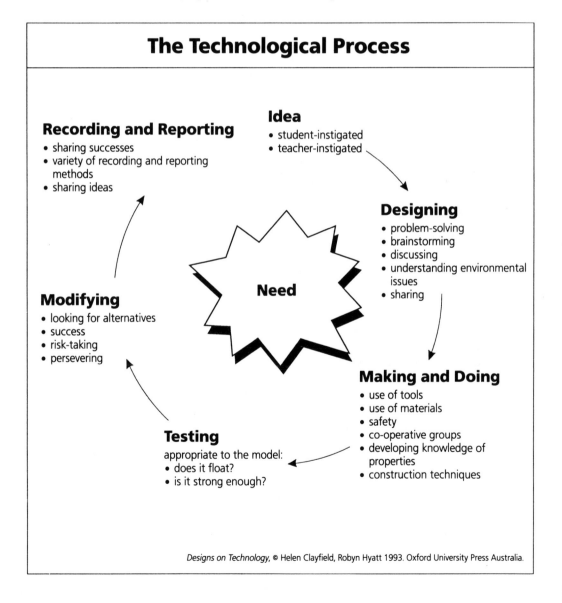

The Technological Process

Recording and Reporting
- sharing successes
- variety of recording and reporting methods
- sharing ideas

Idea
- student-instigated
- teacher-instigated

Designing
- problem-solving
- brainstorming
- discussing
- understanding environmental issues
- sharing

Modifying
- looking for alternatives
- success
- risk-taking
- persevering

Need

Making and Doing
- use of tools
- use of materials
- safety
- co-operative groups
- developing knowledge of properties
- construction techniques

Testing
appropriate to the model:
- does it float?
- is it strong enough?

Designs on Technology, © Helen Clayfield, Robyn Hyatt 1993. Oxford University Press Australia.

Literacy Learning and Technology

An added bonus of technology in the classroom is the language-learning that is generated. Sessions can be planned to incorporate a balance of reading, writing and speaking skills that complement existing classroom programs. Among these are:

- modelling and demonstration
- research skills
- recording information in a variety of ways:
  — note taking
  — surveys
  — diagrams
  — tables
  — questionnaires
  — technology log/journal
  — photographs/labelling
  — audio/video tape
- labelling for both reading and writing
- public speaking— verbal reporting to others—writing notes/reports
- brainstorming techniques which leads on to concept maps, discussion, the clarification of ideas and the sharing of information (conferencing)
- comprehension which leads to the understanding and interpreting of problems
- correct terminology which leads to vocabulary development
- following written instructions
- styles of writing
- drafts
- literature—use of a book to introduce an activity.

Approaches to Organisation

Technology allows teachers to utilise many different approaches, methods and management techniques which contribute to the success of the program. Below is a list of approaches that can be used according to the needs of the students and the nature of the topic.

Student Organisation
- Whole class
  — all the students use the same design brief

- Small groups
  - — 1 × 4 activities — small groups all do the same activity
  - — students work together co-operatively using the same design brief
  - — four activities — each group is allocated a different activity
- Partners
  - — students work with a partner on self-initiated or teacher-initiated design briefs
- Individuals
  - — students work alone on self-initiated or teacher-initiated design briefs
- Cross-age tutoring
  - — students of different grade levels work together to complete design briefs

Projects

- After becoming familiar with the process, students can be actively involved in planning their own technology projects.

Time Allocation

Flexibility is the key here.

- Some tasks can be completed in one short session, others will be part of a series of sessions. For example, sessions may be undertaken on a daily basis over a five-day period or once a week for five weeks.
- You may choose to rearrange your weekly timetable to enable a half or full day to be devoted entirely to technology.
- Technology may be the curriculum focus for an integrated unit of work which may be for a week, a month or a term.

Teacher Organisation

- Depending on staffing arrangements at your school and/or availability of members of the school community, some of the following may be suitable for your class:
  - — team-teaching
  - — work with the specialist teachers for a unit of work
  - — have a specialist technology teacher
  - — share expertise, for example, swap grades for different subjects
  - — invite experts in their field to participate in units of work, for example, a bootmaker
  - — invite members of the school community to help by donating items or assisting during lessons.

Resource Organisation

There are many options for organising resources. Easy access to materials is important, therefore a portable technology box for each classroom containing expendable items such as tape, glue, assorted pins, rubber bands, straws, wire, string and balsa-wood, is of great value.

Classrooms usually have a set of basic equipment such as scissors, staplers, Stanley Knife, which can be used in conjunction with the box.

Specialised equipment such as saws, hammers, drills and chisels are best kept in a safe storage area and borrowed when necessary. Arrangements could be made to use equipment and tools already housed within the school, for example, in the art room.

For some schools it may be more practical to set up a technology trolley to house all equipment and materials. This can be moved to classrooms as required. Central storage is another option which allows teachers to gather items when they are needed.

Large garbage bins can be used to store bulky materials.

Shopping List

This is an extensive list of items that may be used in a technology program.

Adhesives

- ☐ PVA
- ☐ Araldite
- ☐ Tarzan's Grip
- ☐ Contact Cement
- ☐ Hobby Glue
- ☐ Glu-Stik
- ☐ Clag
- ☐ Superglue
- ☐ double-sided tape
- ☐ insulation tape
- ☐ packaging tape
- ☐ wallpaper paste
- ☐ sticky tape (assorted widths)
- ☐ masking tape (assorted widths)
- ☐ Blu-tak

Pins/Nails/Screws

- ☐ drawing-pins
- ☐ glass headed pins
- ☐ dressmaking pins
- ☐ split pins (assorted sizes)
- ☐ nails and screws (assorted lengths and thicknesses)
- ☐ darning needles
- ☐ bodkins

Threads

- ☐ jute
- ☐ string (assorted ply)
- ☐ wool (assorted ply)
- ☐ fishing line
- ☐ sewing cotton
- ☐ macrame string
- ☐ rope

Cardboard/Paper

- ☐ corrugated cardboard
- ☐ brown paper
- ☐ cartridge paper
- ☐ egg-cartons
- ☐ cover paper
- ☐ boxes
- ☐ coloured paper squares, circles
- ☐ crepe paper
- ☐ butcher's paper
- ☐ computer paper (recycled)
- ☐ cellophane
- ☐ tracing paper
- ☐ milk-cartons
- ☐ paper plates
- ☐ sandpaper
- ☐ newspaper
- ☐ wallpaper sample books

Wire

- ☐ florist's wire
- ☐ copper wire
- ☐ coathangers
- ☐ wire (assorted guages)
- ☐ plastic bag ties (coated wire) of assorted lengths
- ☐ plastic-coated wire (for use with circuits)

Batteries

- ☐ 6 volt batteries

Plastics/Rubber

- ☐ bottles
- ☐ foam rubber
- ☐ drinking straws
- ☐ polystyrene (for example, food trays and packaging materials)
- ☐ laminex samples
- ☐ perspex samples
- ☐ jar lids
- ☐ rubber bands (assorted sizes)
- ☐ garbage bags
- ☐ food wrap

Fabric (off-cuts and samples)

- ☐ fake fur
- ☐ sheepskin
- ☐ hessian
- ☐ cotton
- ☐ felt
- ☐ leather
- ☐ calico
- ☐ canvas
- ☐ netting
- ☐ vinyl (samples and off-cuts)
- ☐ furnishing fabric sample books
- ☐ shademesh
- ☐ netting

Wood

- ☐ balsa-wood (available in packs from art suppliers) assorted sizes and thicknesses
- ☐ icy-pole sticks
- ☐ off-cuts of a variety of woods such as chipboard, ply, pine or masonite
- ☐ skewers
- ☐ bamboo sticks

Tools/Equipment

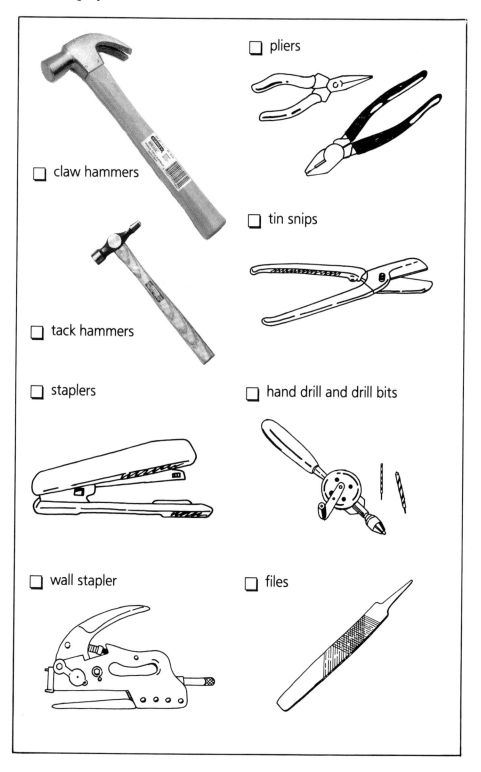

☐ claw hammers

☐ tack hammers

☐ staplers

☐ wall stapler

☐ pliers

☐ tin snips

☐ hand drill and drill bits

☐ files

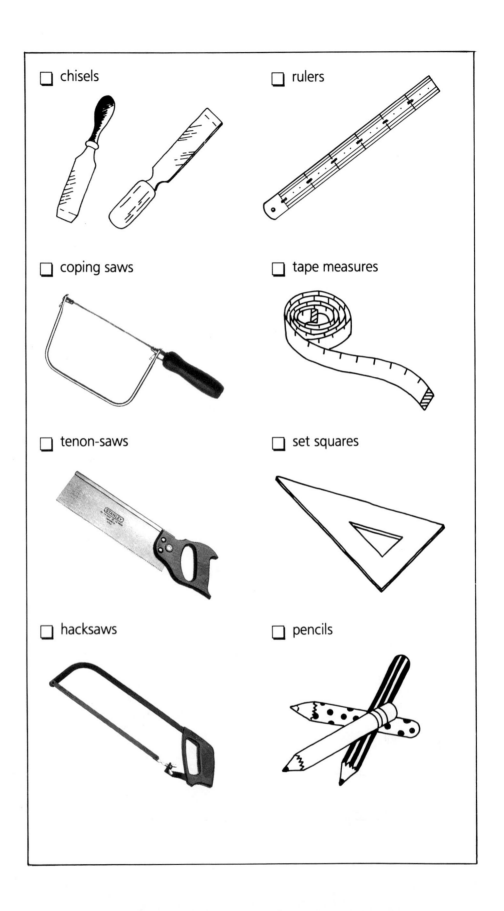

- [ ] chisels
- [ ] rulers
- [ ] coping saws
- [ ] tape measures
- [ ] tenon-saws
- [ ] set squares
- [ ] hacksaws
- [ ] pencils

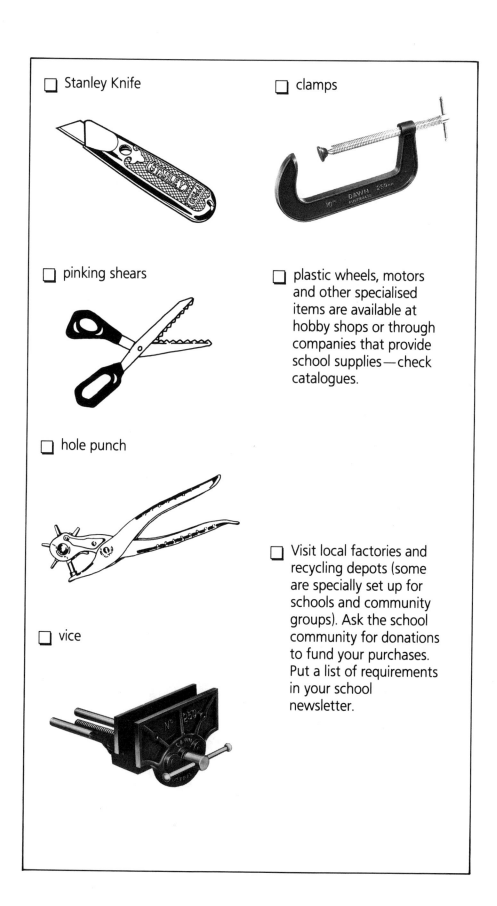

☐ Stanley Knife

☐ clamps

☐ pinking shears

☐ plastic wheels, motors and other specialised items are available at hobby shops or through companies that provide school supplies—check catalogues.

☐ hole punch

☐ Visit local factories and recycling depots (some are specially set up for schools and community groups). Ask the school community for donations to fund your purchases. Put a list of requirements in your school newsletter.

☐ vice

Safety

Teachers are responsible for providing a safe working environment for their students. It is important therefore to use appropriate equipment for tasks.

- Ensure equipment and tools are in good condition.
- Demonstrate safe use of equipment and tools.
- Discuss product labels and symbols, for example, on glues and paints.
- Use gloves and protective clothing if necessary.
- Ventilate areas when gluing.
- Enlist extra adults for tasks needing closer supervision or when young students are learning how to use unfamiliar equipment.
- Ensure students have enough room to work.
- Cut cords from non-working electrical items before allowing students to tinker with them.

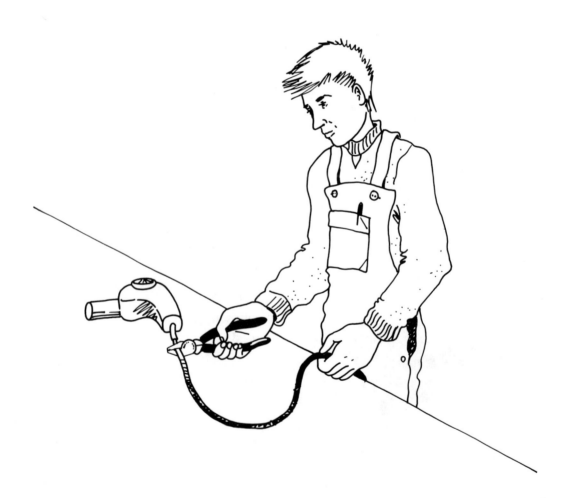

Recording and Reporting

There are many ways students can record and report outcomes of their technology investigations, here are a few examples.

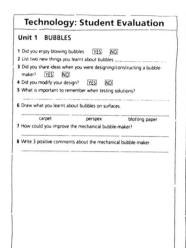

Technology: Student Evaluation

Unit 1   BUBBLES

1 Did you enjoy blowing bubbles   YES   NO

2 List two new things you learnt about bubbles _____

3 Did you share ideas when you were designing/constructing a bubble-maker?   YES   NO

4 Did you modify your design?   YES   NO

5 What is important to remember when testing solutions?

6 Draw what you learnt about bubbles on surfaces.

    carpet   perspex   blotting paper

7 How could you improve the mechanical bubble-maker?

8 Write 3 positive comments about the mechanical bubble-maker.

Bubble Experiments

Carpet
Prediction:
We predict that bubbles will pop when they land on carpet. They'll pop because the bubbles are light and thin and the carpet is rough.
Outcome:
The bubbles bounced on carpet.

Blotting Paper
Prediction:
The blotting paper is thick and rough.
We predict the paper will get wet.
The majority of the class predicts that the bubbles will get wet and stay on the paper.
Outcome:
The bubbles popped on blotting paper.

Perspex
Prediction:
8 people predict the bubbles will pop on perspex.
14 people predict that the bubbles will just sit on the perspex.
Outcome:
The bubbles sat on the perspex in semi-spheres.

Laminex
Prediction:
The laminex is smooth and slippery.
We predict the bubbles will stay on the laminex.
Outcome:
The bubbles slid around on the laminex.

Bubble-makers

Your task is to construct at least four different bubble-makers using a variety of materials.

List the materials and equipment you used

Which bubblemaker was the most successful?

Why?

Did you modify any of your designs? Which one and how?

Draw a diagram of each bubble-maker and indicate its success rate from 1–5.

I used a

tube and cotton reel

plastic net

straw with lots of cuts

straw with sticky tape half way along

The plastic net was the most successful

Because it has lots of holes and they joined together.

No I didn't

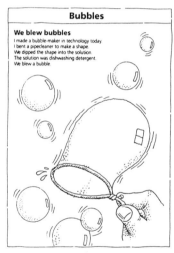

Bubbles

We blew bubbles
I made a bubble-maker in technology today.
I bent a pipecleaner to make a shape.
We dipped the shape into the solution.
The solution was dishwashing detergent.
We blew a bubble.

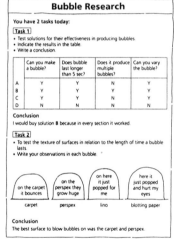

Bubble Research

You have 2 tasks today:

Task 1
• Test solutions for their effectiveness in producing bubbles.
• Indicate the results in the table.
• Write a conclusion.

	Can you make a bubble?	Does bubble last longer than 5 sec?	Does it produce multiple bubbles?	Can you vary the bubble?
A	Y	Y	N	Y
B	Y	Y	Y	Y
C	Y	Y	N	Y
D	N	N	N	N

Conclusion
I would buy solution B because in every section it worked.

Task 2
• To test the texture of surfaces in relation to the length of time a bubble lasts.
• Write your observations in each bubble.

on the carpet it bounces	on the perspex they grow huge	on here it just popped for me	here it just popped and hurt my eyes
carpet	perspex	lino	blotting paper

Conclusion
The best surface to blow bubbles on was the carpet and perspex.

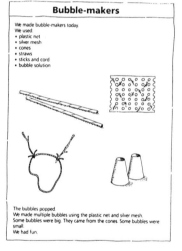

Bubble-makers

We made bubble-makers today.
We used:
• plastic net
• silver mesh
• cones
• straws
• sticks and cord
• bubble solution

The bubbles popped
We made multiple bubbles using the plastic net and silver mesh.
Some bubbles were big. They came from the cones. Some bubbles were small.
We had fun.

How to use this Book

The twenty-four units of work provide a starting-point for technology in the classroom. Each unit provides opportunities for students to explore all the elements of the technology process: designing and making, testing and modifying, and recording and reporting. We have included a variety of topics to maintain interest and broaden students' knowledge. The units are self-contained and can be used by themselves or can be incorporated easily into integrated themes. A sample of an integrated unit is shown below. Units may be adapted to suit any year level.

Materials and equipment suggested in each design brief are generally available in schools or are easily obtainable. Commercial kits such as Lego and Meccano can be valuable additions to the technology program. There are kits appropriate for all age levels, for example, Torro, with large pieces, is ideal for younger students. All of these kits can be used to complement units of work, as part of a series of rotational activities or as free exploration activities.

Curriculum Planner—Integrated Unit

Language—English
- Read other books about pigs, such as Anthony Browne's *Piggybook*.
- Rhyming words: fig, big, gig, dig, wig, jig
- Read other stories about 3s, e.g. *Goldilocks and the Three Bears*.
- Research the origins of '3' stories.
- Tri = three, what other words have this prefix?

Personal Development
- Living together co-operatively—could it have saved the pigs?
- Could the wolf have been a friend?
- Caring for people, e.g. Safety House Programmes.

Social Education
- Research how early homes were built.
- Religious mores—sacred animals
- Research a piggery.
- What has happened to the wild animals of the world?
- Wild pigs/boars—destroying native flora/fauna

Technology—The Three Little Pigs
- Construct a house for the three little pigs.
- Investigate methods of construction/joining materials.
- Design more appropriate homes for the three pigs.
- Testing: Simulate the wolf's breath.

Evaluation
- Have students constructed houses that can withstand the wolf's breath?
- Can they tell why?
- Get students to test what they have learnt during the unit.

Mathematics
- Count by threes.
- Triangles
- Cost of homes and construction materials
- Triangular numbers

3   6   10   15

Resources
- Adhesives
- Junk material
- Straws, pins, popsticks
- Books about 'The Three Little Pigs'
- Photos, posters of a variety of house designs

Science
- Make glue from flour and water and test its adhesive qualities on different materials.
- Make up batches of plaster or cement to discover its properties—try different mixes/strengths.

The Arts
- Design furnishings to complement the exterior construction.
- Create a model of a landscape containing the three houses.
- Produce a play of the story complete with sets, music, etc.

Commerce
- Produce a brochure extolling the virtues of each kind of home.

It is important for students to gain an understanding of technology from an historical perspective, so we have included some background information that will be of interest to both you and your students.

Recording and reporting are essential elements in the process. Some recording sheets are provided and suggestions on other ways of recording and reporting are supplied.

A selection of activities for broadening the unit is included in the section called 'Further Investigations'.

Evaluation is an ongoing process and teachers need to make observations of the students as they proceed through the units. At the end of each unit teachers may develop focus questions based on the skills and techniques explored, in order to assess their students.

Materials

Bubbles

Students will investigate how bubbles are made and apply this knowledge to make bubble-makers. They will experiment with a variety of materials and determine which ones will withstand a soapy solution.

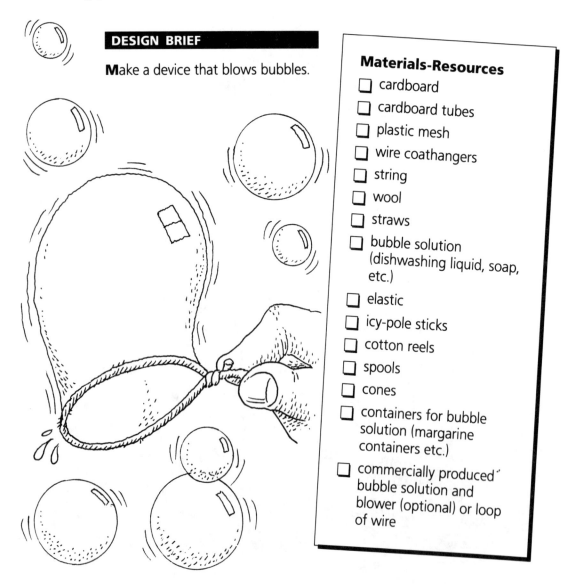

Materials-Resources
- [ ] cardboard
- [ ] cardboard tubes
- [ ] plastic mesh
- [ ] wire coathangers
- [ ] string
- [ ] wool
- [ ] straws
- [ ] bubble solution (dishwashing liquid, soap, etc.)
- [ ] elastic
- [ ] icy-pole sticks
- [ ] cotton reels
- [ ] spools
- [ ] cones
- [ ] containers for bubble solution (margarine containers etc.)
- [ ] commercially produced bubble solution and blower (optional) or loop of wire

TEACHING POINTS

This activity is best done out of the classroom as the surfaces where students work can become very soapy.

Students should blow a bubble using the bubble blower or loop of wire, then dip a U-shaped piece of wire into the solution and try to blow a bubble. Do this several times.

Ask students why the U-shaped wire did not produce a bubble, list responses and discuss.

Ask students to describe the shape of the bubble-makers that they have seen.

Let students experiment with the available materials and bubble solutions to produce bubbles. Make bubbles using hands.

RECORDING AND REPORTING

Students sketch and label their designs, rating which designs worked the best and why.

FURTHER INVESTIGATIONS

Make up different strengths of bubble solution and test using the same bubble-maker. Fill in results on a recording sheet.

Design and make a mechanical bubble-maker.

Make a giant bubble-maker to produce giant bubbles.

Make a bubble-maker to produce multiple bubbles.

Investigate blowing bubbles on different surfaces (for example, on a shiny surface, carpet, paper, water) and record your observations.

bubble solution

Students should design several bubble-makers and test. Encourage students to use different materials in each one.

Did you know?

Soap has been known for at least 2300 years. The Phoenicians prepared it from goats' tallow and wood ashes in 600 BC. The Celts produced their soap from animal fats and plant ashes and named the produce 'saipo' from which the word soap is derived.

Junk Castle

Students will investigate methods of construction and how recycled materials can be used with imagination and creativity.

DESIGN BRIEF

Make a junk castle. The design should include a drawbridge, a moat, and windows and doors that open and shut.

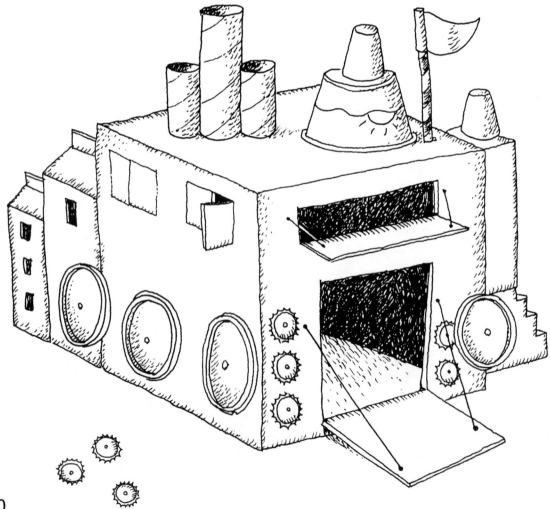

20

Materials-Resources

- ☐ copy of *Junk Castle* written by Robin Klein
- ☐ large and small cardboard boxes
- ☐ cardboard of different thicknesses
- ☐ cardboard tubes and rolls
- ☐ egg-cartons
- ☐ milk-cartons
- ☐ adhesive tape
- ☐ string
- ☐ twine
- ☐ wire
- ☐ art materials
- ☐ pins
- ☐ split pins
- ☐ wood off-cuts
- ☐ glue
- ☐ balsa-wood
- ☐ rubber bands
- ☐ straws
- ☐ hole punch

Read the story over a few days.

Discuss the issues involved in the book, for example, lack of playing space in inner urban areas, solving problems by compromise, etc.

Discuss the features of the 'junk castle' as described in the book.

Sketch a drawbridge on butcher's paper and ask students to suggest possible ways of raising and lowering the bridge using available materials.

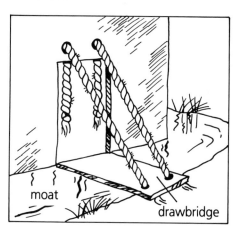

moat

drawbridge

Give students time to imagine and then sketch what they think the 'junk castle' would look like.

Students should make decisions about how the task will be undertaken, for example, will it be a class project with one large castle being constructed, small group work, or individuals working alone to construct a small model.

Students should select materials that are appropriate to the way they are working.

If students choose to make one large castle, a large working area needs to be available, this project may then extend over several days.

RECORDING AND REPORTING

Take photographs of the completed castle.

Students should make an advertising poster highlighting the features of their 'junk castle', and include a photograph.

Did you know?
The largest inhabited castle in the world is the royal residence of Windsor Castle in Berkshire, England.

FURTHER INVESTIGATIONS

Read other Robin Klein novels.

Investigate housing that uses recycled materials.

Plan a balcony garden for someone living in a high-rise apartment.

Research the history of a famous castle, for example, Windsor Castle in England, and present the history as a project.

Retell the story of *Junk Castle*, using different characters in a different time and place.

Read the book *My Place* by Nadia Wheatly and think about the changes that occur in the neighbourhood over time.

My Place by Nadia Wheatley (Collins Dove, 1987).

Musical Instruments

Students will investigate how sound is produced and apply this knowledge to make their own instruments.

DESIGN BRIEF

Make an instrument that produces sound.

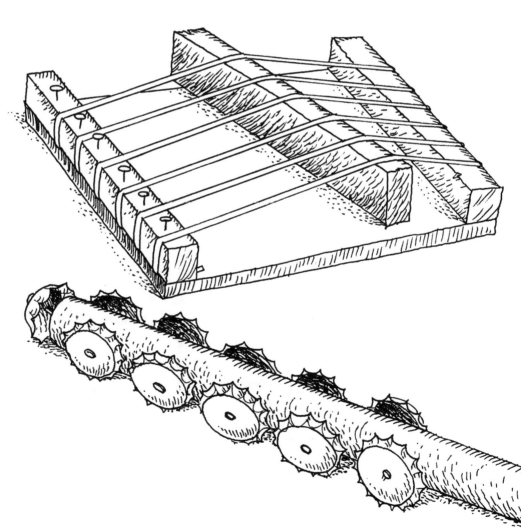

Materials-Resources

- [ ] tins
- [ ] balloons
- [ ] rubber-bands
- [ ] jars
- [ ] bottle tops
- [ ] string
- [ ] assorted boxes and plastic bottles
- [ ] wire
- [ ] bamboo
- [ ] cardboard tubes
- [ ] pipe
- [ ] nails
- [ ] hammers
- [ ] seeds
- [ ] rice
- [ ] assorted adhesive tapes and glue
- [ ] records or tapes of music from various countries, for example, Scottish bagpipes, South American pipes, Indian sitar
- [ ] posters or photographs of a selection of tuned and untuned instruments, try to include uncommon instruments if possible
- [ ] a selection of instruments for student use, for example, recorders, drums, toneblocks and tambourines
- [ ] blank tape and cassette recorder

TEACHING POINTS

Before you begin the activity, play a selection of music to students and discuss the types of instruments used to create the different sounds.

Discuss with students how instruments can be classified into groups: wind, percussion, string, brass.

Demonstrate how sound is produced, for example, tapping a balloon stretched over a hollow container, blowing through a hollow tube, etc.

Allow students in small groups to make sounds using the instruments provided. Direct them to look at the way in which the instrument has been constructed, and the materials used.

continued

As a class, discuss what the students have observed, students are then able to classify the instruments according to how sound is produced, the materials used, etc.

Students construct instruments using the materials provided.

This activity is bound to be noisy so try to arrange a time or place that will not disrupt other classes.

Encourage students to be creative in making non-conventional looking instruments.

RECORDING AND REPORTING

Students play their instruments to the class.

These presentations could be taped, along with a commentary of the process of making the instrument.

Make a labelled sketch of the instrument and how the sound is produced.

FURTHER INVESTIGATIONS

Make a bush band.

Invite a bush band, orchestra or trio to play for the class.

Choose an instrument to research and present the information in project form.

Research a famous musician or composer.

Investigate how a compact disc player or a cassette player works.

Conduct a survey to determine the most popular songs in the class or school. Present the information in graph form.

Did you know?

Wolfgang Amadeus Mozart wrote 1000 operas, operettas, symphonies, violin sonatas, divertimenti, serenades, concertos for piano and many other instruments, string quartets, other chamber music, masses and litanies, of which only seventy were published, before he died at the age of thirty-five.

Slipper Sock

Students will investigate stitching as a method of joining materials.

Make a pair of slipper socks.

Materials-Resources
- ☐ pair of knee-high socks
- ☐ vinyl fabric (cut into pieces large enough for each student's slippers)
- ☐ darning needles
- ☐ wool
- ☐ hole punch
- ☐ pins
- ☐ cardboard
- ☐ instruction sheet (one for each student)

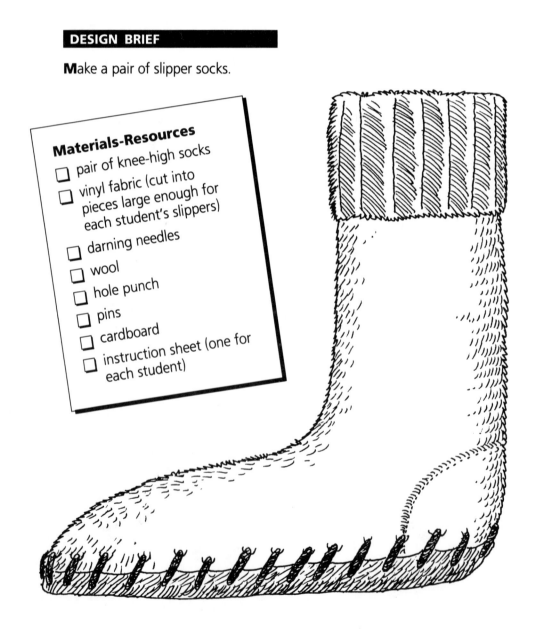

TEACHING POINTS

Demonstrate the making of a slipper sock following the instruction sheet.

Provide students with samples of vinyl and old socks so they can practise skills such as hole punching and sewing.

When students are confident with their skills they make the slipper socks.

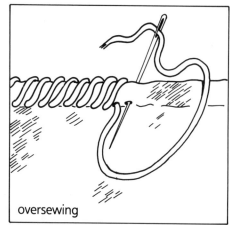
oversewing

hole punch

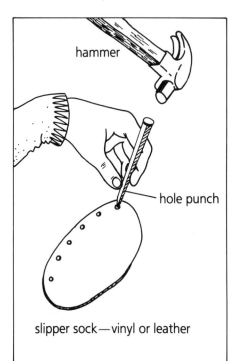
hammer

hole punch

slipper sock—vinyl or leather

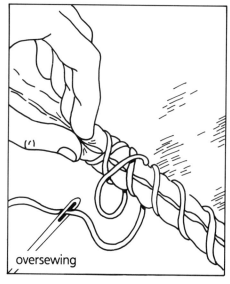
oversewing

This is a great activity to involve extra adults to help the students.

RECORDING AND REPORTING

Arrange a parade of slipper socks with a commentary.

Draw and label the slipper sock using accurate details, for example, the colour and pattern of the sock.

Instructions to make Slipper Socks

1 Put your socks on and stand on the cardboard. Mark the length and width of each foot.

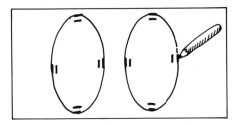

2 Add 1 cm to each mark and join the marks together to form an oval shape.

3 Make sure you label the left and right foot.

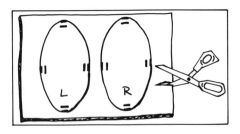

4 Cut out the template and place on the vinyl, trace around and cut out.

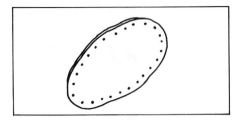

5 Mark holes approximately 1 cm apart all around the vinyl.

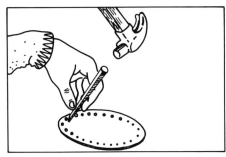

6 Use the marks as guides to make the holes with the hole punch.

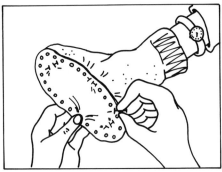

7 With a partner's help, pin the vinyl to the sole of the sock.

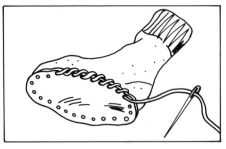

8 Stitch the vinyl to the sock using the wool.

9 Secure firmly before knotting and cutting the wool.

Invite a shoemaker to a class.

Read *The Elves and the Shoemaker*.

Study footwear through the ages.

Design footwear for a specific purpose, for example, shoes for a slippery surface.

Investigate footwear from different countries and present in project form.

Did you know?
Cinderella's slipper in the original story was not made of glass, but of fur.

Tactile Mural

Students will investigate the properties of materials and the use of appropriate tools.

DESIGN BRIEF

Create a mural using items that are found around the home and school. The items must be altered in some way, for example, cut or folded, and safely attached to the mural. People must be able to *feel* the mural without danger.

Materials-Resources

Only materials which are safe should be used, these include:

- ☐ cans
- ☐ egg-cartons
- ☐ plastic bottles
- ☐ lids
- ☐ carpet pieces
- ☐ fabric
- ☐ envelopes
- ☐ leather
- ☐ pine-cones
- ☐ feathers
- ☐ foil
- ☐ pasta
- ☐ sandpaper
- ☐ paint
- ☐ variety of adhesives
- ☐ tin snips
- ☐ scissors
- ☐ pinking shears
- ☐ saws
- ☐ hammers
- ☐ nails

continued

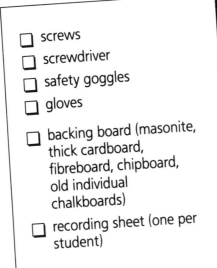

- ☐ screws
- ☐ screwdriver
- ☐ safety goggles
- ☐ gloves
- ☐ backing board (masonite, thick cardboard, fibreboard, chipboard, old individual chalkboards)
- ☐ recording sheet (one per student)

To create an artistic effect, the mural could be hand or spray painted (if spray painting, take the mural outside on a still day and wear appropriate protective gear, it may be best for the teacher or adult to do this part of the mural).

RECORDING AND REPORTING

Complete the recording sheet.

Display the mural and invite people to feel it.

FURTHER INVESTIGATIONS

Research and present a project showing the manufacturing process of something that is on the mural.

Encourage the students to write to companies requesting brochures and pamphlets illustrating the manufacturing process of something used on the mural.

Create specific murals, for example, smooth textures, rough textures, all natural, etc.

Research the Iron Age, Bronze Age, etc.

Investigate a specific material such as glass, its development, its use both practical and artistic.

TEACHING POINTS

Reinforce safety procedures for using adhesives and tools before you begin. The mural must be safe to feel, there should not be any sharp edges.

Allow the students time to become familiar with the textures of the materials and then discuss their properties and origin, for example, in their natural state, processed or synthetic, and ways of attaching them to the backing board.

Discuss the options for the mural, for example, will there be a large class mural or several small group murals that can be joined together.

Did you know?
Murals have existed since cave-dwellers marked walls with natural paints.

Tactile Mural

R

Name: _____

Item	man made	natural	tactile description	method of attachment	tools used
Sheepskin		√	furry soft	PVA glue	scissors
Bottle top	√		hard, rigid round	nails	hammer
Egg-carton	√		bumpy fibrous	masking tape	scissors Stanley knife

Key-ring

Students will investigate the properties of plastics and the use of appropriate tools to make a practical item.

DESIGN BRIEF

Design and make a key-ring using plastic as the main material.

Materials-Resources

- [ ] plastic off-cuts of different thicknesses
- [ ] perspex
- [ ] variety of adhesives (PVA, Tarzan's Grip, bonding cement, plastic glue, Araldite)
- [ ] files
- [ ] hand drills
- [ ] coping saws (well-sharpened)
- [ ] hacksaw blades
- [ ] coarse sandpaper
- [ ] metal key-rings

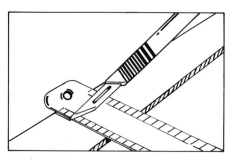

scoring

snapping

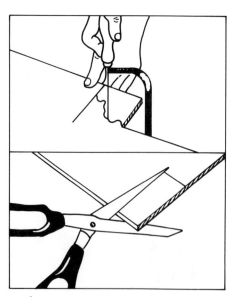

cutting

TEACHING POINTS

Collect examples of a variety of plastics used in everyday products.

Brainstorm, then list the properties of plastics, for example, smooth, see-through, hard or shiny. Discuss these properties, comparing them with other materials such as wood or metal.

Demonstrate scoring and snapping, and cutting and shaping using the appropriate tools.

Investigate how plastics may be joined together using different types of adhesives.

Allow students the opportunity to experiment and work with the plastic scraps.

Students design and make a key-ring based on simple shapes and using the techniques demonstrated. Shapes may be overlapped to add interest and then joined together using suitable glue. Attach metal ring when completed.

RECORDING AND REPORTING

Students list and draw the tools, glues and materials they used.

FURTHER INVESTIGATIONS

Research recycling, and find out which plastics can be recycled.

Investigate the uses of plastics in the home and present as a project.

Write to plastic manufacturers for information on how plastics are made and how plastic products are manufactured.

Use liquid plastic, available from hobby shops, to embed items.

Did you know?

Wallace Carothers, an American chemist, produced a plastic called 'nylon' in 1934. It was like artificial silk and could be drawn out into thin threads and woven into cloth.

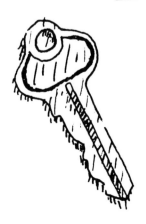

Bird Feeder

Students will investigate the use of tools, how to follow instructions and use a pattern.

DESIGN BRIEF

Construct a hanging bird feeder.

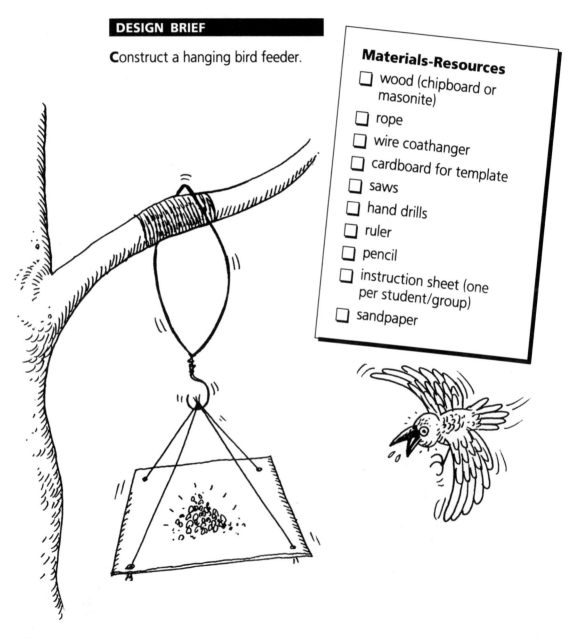

Materials-Resources

- [ ] wood (chipboard or masonite)
- [ ] rope
- [ ] wire coathanger
- [ ] cardboard for template
- [ ] saws
- [ ] hand drills
- [ ] ruler
- [ ] pencil
- [ ] instruction sheet (one per student/group)
- [ ] sandpaper

TEACHING POINTS

Make square cardboard templates 30 cm × 30 cm.

Demonstrate how to use a saw and a hand drill safely, and provide opportunities for students to practise on scraps before starting on the design brief.

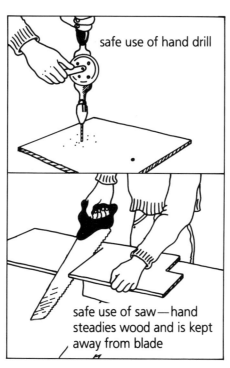

safe use of hand drill

safe use of saw—hand steadies wood and is kept away from blade

Provide a copy of the instruction sheet to each student or group of students and read together.

Discuss the most practical placement of the template on the wood to minimise wastage.

Observe students to ensure that the tools are being used correctly, and give assistance where needed.

Discuss the need to have the ropes of equal length and knots tied at approximately the same place. You may have to demonstrate the correct technique of tying a knot.

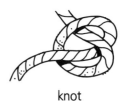

knot

For younger children, make the feeder from cardboard using the same instructions and use a hole punch for the holes instead of drilling.

To prevent the weight of the bird feeder damaging the tree, place fabric between the branch and the wire.

RECORDING AND REPORTING

Draw and label the tools used.

List the safety rules followed.

Did you know?

The house sparrow, starling and myna are not native Australian birds. They were introduced into Australia in the 1860s.

FURTHER INVESTIGATIONS

Prepare feed mixture using a recipe.

Design a variety of bird feeders for different situations, for example, caged birds.

Design and make an automatic feeder.

Investigate the types of birds that live near the school.

Plant bird-attracting shrubs and trees.

Design and build a free-standing bird platform.

Design a feeder with a removable dish.

Instructions for Bird Feeder

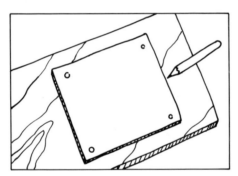

1 Place the template on the wood and trace around the edges of the square and the holes.

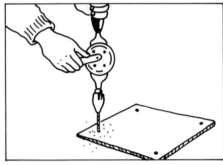

3 Drill the holes where marked.

4 Sand the rough edges with sandpaper.

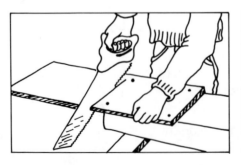

2 Saw along the lines.

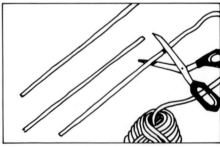

5 Measure and cut four pieces of string 60 cm long.

6 Tie several knots at the end of each piece of rope.

7 Thread the rope through the holes so that the knots are underneath.

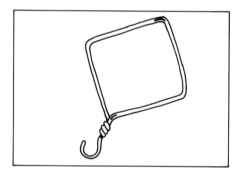

8 Bend the coathanger.

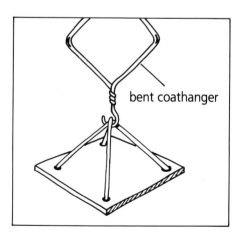

bent coathanger

9 Tie diagonally opposite ropes together over the hook.

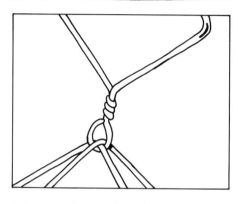

10 Bend the hook to form a loop to prevent the rope falling off.

pad or cloth to protect branch

hanger is looped over end of sturdy branch

11 Slip the coathanger over a medium-weight branch of a tree.

Parachutes

Students will investigate the properties of materials and make decisions about the most appropriate material for the task.

DESIGN BRIEF

Make mini-parachutes using a variety of materials. Test to determine which materials produce the best result.

Materials-Resources

- ☐ parachute pattern
- ☐ string or wool
- ☐ parachutist template
- ☐ Textas
- ☐ adhesive tape
- ☐ hole punch
- ☐ blackboard ruler
- ☐ copy of recording sheet
- ☐ a variety of materials of different weight and density such as newspaper, cotton fabric, plastic garbage bag, tissue paper, plastic film and pantihose

Select three or four different types of materials from those available, making sure to include at least one that is light-weight.

Brainstorm all the facts students know about parachutes.

Before making the parachutes, make predictions about the materials in terms of which will give the best results and why. Determine criteria on which to base the results of the test, for example, a good parachute takes the longest time to reach the ground, drops smoothly etc.

Class organisation for this activity can be varied depending on the age level of students and the time available.

20 cm

20 cm

For younger children it may be more convenient to make up test parachutes, record students' predictions, then test. Students then make their own parachutes and test.

In order to give a good test, it is desirable that parachutes are launched from a reasonable height. Students can be elevated by standing on the top of outside steps, a stable chair, or playground equipment. Alternatively hanging the parachute from the top of the blackboard ruler, held almost vertically by a student, and then released works well.

RECORDING AND REPORTING

Students record results on recording sheet after each test.

Students share their test results and offer explanations as to the successes of the materials used.

FURTHER INVESTIGATIONS

Students research the origins of the parachute.

Students investigate different types of flight—hang-gliding, parasailing etc.

Students list all the words with the prefix 'para' and give definitions in their own words.

Parachute Template

R

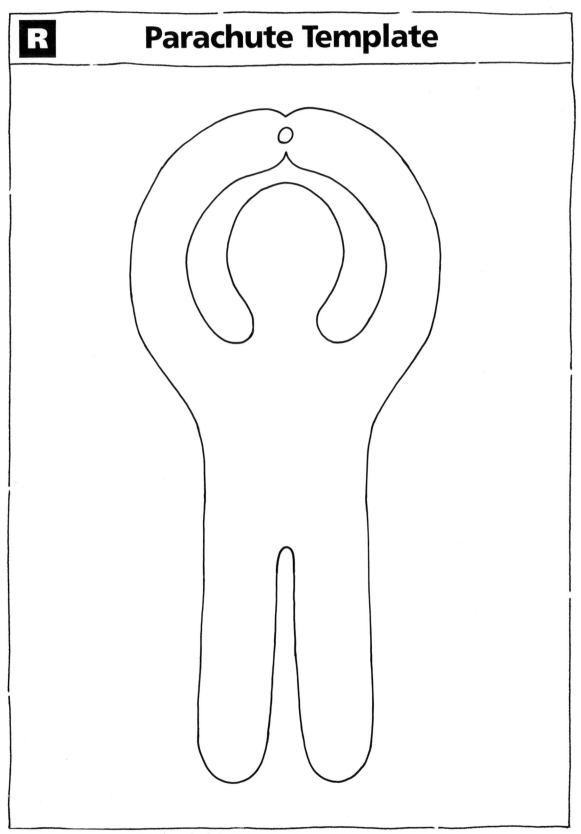

R Parachutes

Name: _____

I predicted _____

_____

_____

Materials used	Result

The parachute constructed using _____

worked the best because _____ .

My prediction was _____

The Three Little Pigs

Students will investigate different methods of construction using a variety of materials.

DESIGN BRIEF

Design and make a house for one of the three little pigs. The house must be able to withstand the breath of the wolf.

Materials-Resources

- ☐ Copy of *The Three Little Pigs* or re-tell the story to the students
- ☐ straws
- ☐ icy-pole sticks
- ☐ cardboard
- ☐ twine or string
- ☐ tape
- ☐ glue
- ☐ plasticine
- ☐ electric fan or hairdryer (for testing)
- ☐ recording sheet

Read or re-tell the story, discussing why the different houses did not stand up to the wolf's huffing and puffing, consider the materials used and the methods of construction.

Before students begin designing their houses, let them experiment with different ways of joining materials. You may wish to direct students to some techniques they may not have considered. Encourage ways of joining without using tape.

Give students the opportunity to share their ideas.

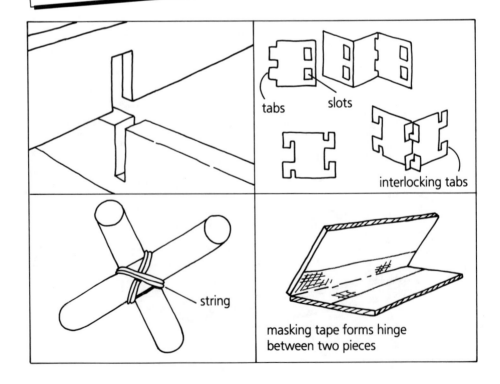

tabs slots

interlocking tabs

string

masking tape forms hinge between two pieces

Students may choose to work in pairs, individually or alternatively in a co-operative group where one model is made.

After the construction stage, test the model houses using the hairdryer or fan to represent the wolf's breath.

Discuss which materials and joining techniques were most suitable for the task.

RECORDING AND REPORTING

Provide one recording sheet for each student or group.

If working in co-operative groups, one group member could report to the whole class on the group's model house.

FURTHER INVESTIGATIONS

Students make a life-size house for the three little pigs, using washed milk-cartons as bricks. Students will need to consider ways of joining the cartons, and ways to include doors, windows and other features.

Students experiment with making 'mud bricks' using a variety of raw materials, and testing for strength and durability.

Take the class to a building site to observe the stages of construction.

Maths link—cost the materials used in the construction of one of the model houses.

Group research—students investigate types of building techniques, for example, wattle and daub.

Did you know?
The wolf has almost been wiped out due to being shot, trapped and poisoned. Wolves prefer to make their dens in holes in the ground, caves or hollow logs not in pigs' houses as the story suggests!

R The Three Little Pigs

Name: _____

☐ I worked alone.

☐ We worked in a group.

Our construction workers were:

_____

_____

This is our house design.

Building materials

_____

_____

_____

_____

Construction technique

_____

_____

_____

_____

TESTING: Rate your design

←——————————————————————————→
0   1   2   3   4   5   6   7   8   9   10

The best feature of the house is _____

_____

I could improve the house by _____

_____

Design

My design for packaging an ice-cream cone

Design F... recipe bo...

My design for a folding chair

Design for my carry bag

Plans for my room cleaner

GOOZIE...

Landmark design

Folding Chair

Students will investigate ways of making movable joints, in relation to the manufacture of furniture.

DESIGN BRIEF

Design and make a folding chair for a doll.

Materials-Resources

- [ ] cardboard
- [ ] balsa-wood
- [ ] wire
- [ ] split pins
- [ ] adhesive tape
- [ ] fabric
- [ ] straws
- [ ] icy-pole sticks
- [ ] glassheaded pins
- [ ] drawing pins
- [ ] scraps of vinyl
- [ ] small doll
- [ ] hole punch
- [ ] either a life-size folding chair, for example deckchair, director's chair or furniture catalogues

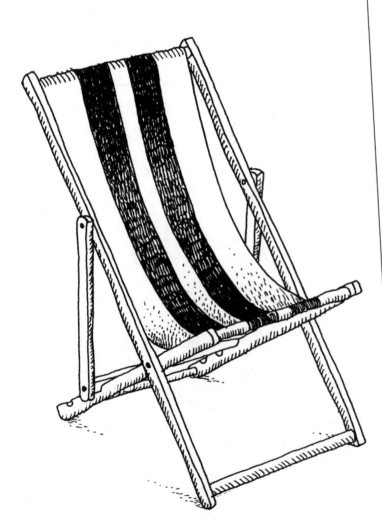

TEACHING POINTS

Show students the chair or the catalogue pictures, discuss the features of the chair that allow it to be folded. Look at the joints and how they are made, and the hardware used.

Use split pins or tape (to resemble hinges) and cardboard strips to demonstrate to students how a long strip can be jointed and folded into a more compact shape.

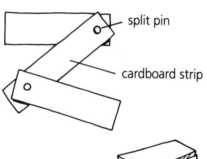

split pin

cardboard strip

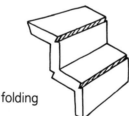

folding

Brainstorm other items that make use of this principle, for example, fold-up tables, prams and strollers.

Allow students time to experiment with the materials provided. Students should then design and construct the fold-up chair.

Students test their design and modify it if required.

RECORDING AND REPORTING

Put each model on display and attach a blank sheet of paper. Students write a constructive comment on each sheet, focusing on the design and the construction technique used.

FURTHER INVESTIGATIONS

Visit a factory and see how furniture is made.

Make a life-size chair based on one of the designs, using appropriate materials and hardware.

Investigate furniture requiring assembly at home. Choose an item and write step by step instructions on how to put it together.

Did you know?

In 1853, Charles Burton patented a collapsible 'hand carriage for children'. It was pushed by a handle from the back. The sides and back of the invention folded down on hinges, the handle screwed off and the two back wheels could be removed.

Food

Students will investigate food design as it relates to technology.

Create an open sandwich that includes ingredients from the five basic good groups. Include foods with a variety of textures and colours, and present the ingredients on the sandwich in an attractive way. The sandwich must be delicious as well!

Materials-Resources

- [ ] posters of the food groups
- [ ] ingredients (depending on what the class is going to make)
- [ ] different varieties of bread
- [ ] chopping boards
- [ ] graters
- [ ] peelers
- [ ] knives
- [ ] spoons
- [ ] paper plates
- [ ] serviettes
- [ ] recipe sheet (one for each student)

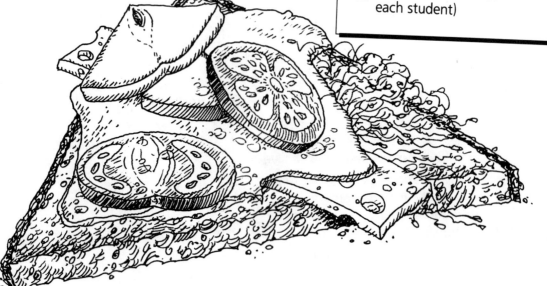

TEACHING POINTS

To complete this activity successfully, students need to have a knowledge of the five basic food groups, so ideally this activity should form part of a unit of work based on food and nutrition.

It is best to do the planning on one day and the making of the sandwich on another, to allow for the ingredients to be purchased or collected.

Prepare a large sheet with the headings of the food groups. Students should list foods that could be used on the sandwich under the appropriate headings. Discuss the foods on the list. You may wish to include other foods here that could be used in the sandwich.

Discuss alternatives, for example, cream cheese could be used instead of butter or margarine.

Students should plan their sandwich considering the food groups, texture, colour and how the sandwich will look and taste.

Students should make a list of the ingredients needed and collate the lists.

Students then prepare the ingredients and make the sandwich.

RECORDING AND REPORTING

Students complete the sandwich recipe sheet.

Students taste a selection of the sandwiches.

FURTHER INVESTIGATIONS

Plan a balanced menu.

Use a pocket calorie counter to plan a meal that contains 6300 kilojoules and includes all of the food groups.

Find out about uncommon fruits and vegetables that students may have seen in the supermarket.

Investigate traditional cooking from other countries and use the recipes to make a cook book.

Did you know?
Hippolyte Mege Mouries invented margarine in 1869 as a substitute for butter.

Super Sandwich

Recipe Sheet

Name: _____

Ingredients used on my super sandwich.

Fruit	Vegetables	Bread Cereals	Meat and alternatives	Diary products

Have you used each of the 5 food groups?   YES ☐   NO ☐

The sandwich tasted _____

The sandwich looked _____

I asked _____ to taste test it.

They said _____

Landmarks

Students will investigate design and methods of construction, and will become aware of the many ways buildings are presented, for example, facade and internal structure.

DESIGN BRIEF

Construct a model of a well-known landmark.

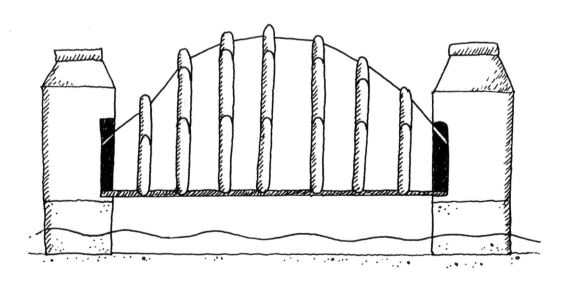

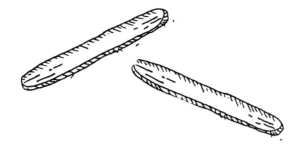

Materials-Resources

- [ ] prints, posters or photographs of well-known landmarks such as: Sydney Harbour Bridge, Opera House, Eiffel Tower, Leaning Tower of Pisa, Great Wall of China
- [ ] cardboard
- [ ] paper
- [ ] assorted adhesive tapes
- [ ] pins
- [ ] staples
- [ ] straws
- [ ] matchsticks
- [ ] icy-pole sticks
- [ ] playdough
- [ ] wire
- [ ] string
- [ ] papier mâché
- [ ] balsa-wood
- [ ] varieties of plastic

TEACHING POINTS

Display images of the landmarks and ask if any students have visited them.

Discuss the obvious or impressive features of the landmarks so that the most suitable materials can be selected to create the models, for example, the Leaning Tower of Pisa could be re-created using a poster tube, and the Sydney Harbour Bridge with matchsticks, straws and playdough.

Allow the students to join materials in a variety of ways, such as folding, looping tape, slotting or flanging, before making their model. (Encourage students to refer to photographs instead of making their own design.)

This activity presents an ideal opportunity for students to work in pairs.

Did you know?

The Sydney Harbour Bridge was built between 1924 and 1932. It spans 503 metres and was built to carry four railway tracks in addition to the roadway and two pedestrian walkways. It was built without using any temporary supports, with the two halves of the bridge built out as cantilevers.

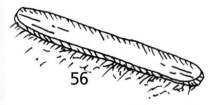

57

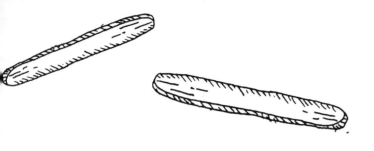

RECORDING AND REPORTING

Display models next to photographs or posters of the real structure.

Students reflect on the likeness of their model to the original.

FURTHER INVESTIGATIONS

Students choose a landmark to investigate.

Students design a landmark with typically Australian characteristics.

Machine of the Future

Students will investigate, design and think about the responsibility of inventions and the needs of humanity.

DESIGN BRIEF

Design a machine of the future.

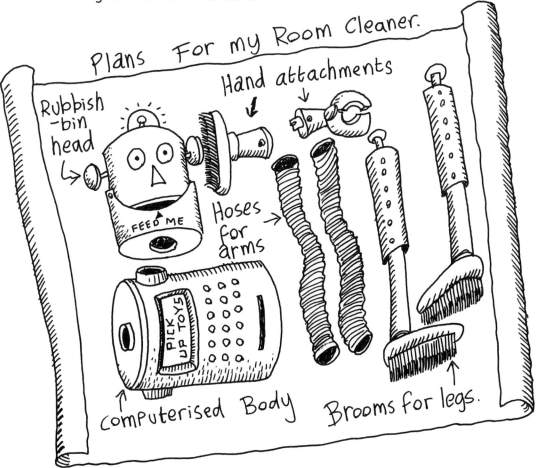

Plans For my Room Cleaner.

Rubbish-bin head →

Hand attachments ↓

FEED ME

Hoses for arms →

PICK UP TOYS

↑ Computerised Body

Brooms for legs. ↑

Materials-Resources

- ☐ paper (butcher's, cartridge)
- ☐ drawing implements
- ☐ rulers
- ☐ set squares
- ☐ templates

Students write a report on how their machine works and why it will be of benefit to society.

These designs could be bound into a class book.

Make up a questionnaire—ask people what things they would like to be done by a machine.

FURTHER INVESTIGATIONS

Students can make a model that looks like their machine.

Research interesting inventions.

TEACHING POINTS

Brainstorm ideas for a futuristic machine that has a positive influence on society. Please remember to value each student's creative ideas.

Allow students time to think about the ideas listed.

Students draw on butcher's paper a number of preliminary sketches for different machines.

In a small group, students present their sketches for discussion and feedback.

Students then select one machine to work on in detail on cartridge paper.

Did you know?

The invention of the typewriter had an unexpected positive influence on society as it contributed to the emancipation of women. When women became typewriter operators they were allowed, for the first time, to work in offices.

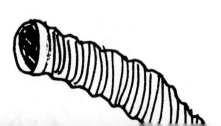

Goozlenut

Students will investigate the relationship between design and the environment.

DESIGN BRIEF

Design and build an all-weather protective structure for 'Goozlenut'.

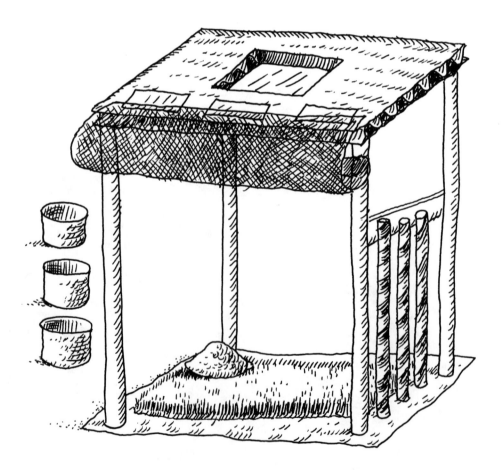

Materials-Resources

- [ ] a 'Goozlenut' for each student or group of students (a gumnut or similar seedpod stuck on a card—use a Texta to draw a nose and eyes to give it character)
- [ ] fabric
- [ ] cardboard
- [ ] plastic
- [ ] foil
- [ ] carpet/vinyl samples
- [ ] string
- [ ] wool
- [ ] grasses/sticks
- [ ] off-cuts of shademesh
- [ ] straws
- [ ] skewers
- [ ] icy-pole sticks
- [ ] stapler
- [ ] assorted adhesive tapes
- [ ] pins
- [ ] photograph album (optional)
- [ ] recording sheet

TEACHING POINTS

Introduce 'Goozlenut' as a creature that needs somewhere to live.

You may like to tell the students a story about 'Goozlenut' or let them make up their own profile (date of birth, place of origin, habitat, food, personality, etc.).

List the features that students think are important for shelter, for example, a roof to keep out the sun and rain.

Provide photos and/or posters of a variety of shelters, for example, pole houses, underground dwellings.

Discuss the things that would need to be considered in an 'environmentally aware' design, such as skylights, transit of sun, shade trees, insulation.

After looking at the available materials, students design and build a shelter for 'Goozlenut'.

RECORDING AND REPORTING

Students complete a recording sheet.

Make a 'Goozlenut' book.

Use a photograph album to display photographs of the completed structures, the design and 'Goozlenut' profiles.

Role Play: be a real estate agent and 'sell' a Goozlenut structure.

FURTHER INVESTIGATIONS

Extend 'Goozlenut's' environment by adding features such as trees, streets and rivers.

Enlarge 'Goozlenut's' structure to accommodate visitors.

Invite an architect to talk to students.

Design a structure for specific conditions, for example, the desert.

Investigate solar power.

Did you know?
A five-star hotel is built underground at the opal mining town of Coober Pedy. People live underground to escape the intense heat.

Goozlenut

Name: _____

This is my design for my Goozlenut shelter.

Side view   Aerial view

Building materials   Construction technique

_____   _____

_____   _____

_____   _____

_____   _____

Packaging

Students will investigate the properties of materials and then make decisions about the most appropriate material for packaging a fragile item.

DESIGN BRIEF

Design and make a package for a fragile item, such as cracker biscuits. Test the effectiveness of the package by dropping it.

Materials-Resources

- [ ] cardboard of different thicknesses
- [ ] paper (newspaper, scrap, computer)
- [ ] polystyrene
- [ ] plastic bags
- [ ] fabric
- [ ] tape
- [ ] adhesives
- [ ] ice-cream cones or cracker biscuits

TEACHING POINTS

Before the lesson, collect samples of a variety of packaging materials, such as Post Paks, shredded paper, polystyrene beads and corrugated cardboard.

Discuss with students how different types of articles are packaged.

Discuss the appropriateness of the material in which ice-cream cones and cracker biscuits are packaged.

Discuss recycling and environmental issues in relation to packaging.

Demonstrate how folded paper and cardboard packaging can lessen the impact on an item that is dropped. Experiment with different folding techniques.

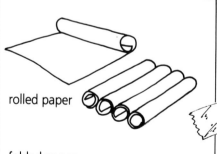

rolled paper

folded paper

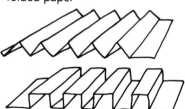

Before making the packaging, students should design a test to determine it effectiveness.

RECORDING AND REPORTING

Students record their design on paper, then report to the class on how the packaging was made and the success of the design.

FURTHER INVESTIGATIONS

Design and make a protective package for an article with an unusual shape.

Students go to a local supermarket and observe the different kinds of packaging used for products, for example, things come in tins, bottles, boxes.

Design packaging that can be recycled and used for another purpose.

Survey—look at a shopping list, and describe the method of packaging of six items on the list.

Did you know?

Before 1800 most people gave unwrapped gifts. The first widely-used gift-wrapping materials were brown paper and twine.

Recipe Book Stand

Students will investigate methods of construction and ways of finding a practical solution to a problem.

DESIGN BRIEF

Design and make a recipe book stand that will stand alone on a bench and allow recipes to be read easily.

Materials-Resources

- ☐ cardboard of different thicknesses
- ☐ cardboard boxes and rolls
- ☐ assorted adhesive tapes
- ☐ string
- ☐ glue
- ☐ split pins
- ☐ rubber bands
- ☐ assorted recipe books for testing

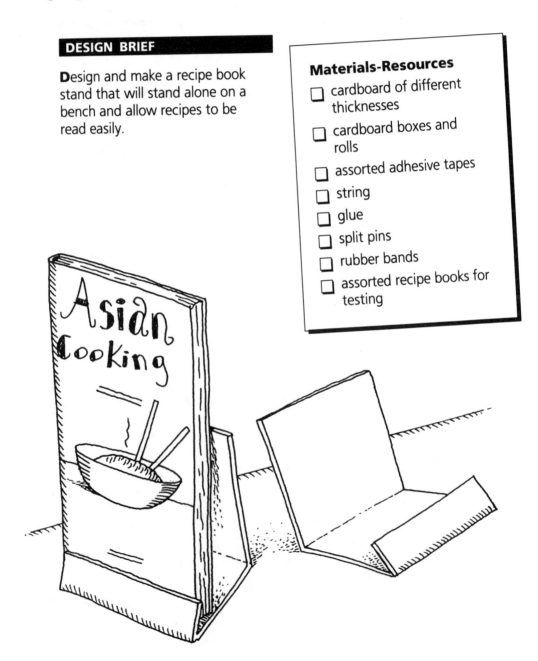

Before you begin, discuss the problem with the students.

Ask students if they have seen book stands in the library, in shops or as advertising displays in supermarkets.

Discuss the key features of a book stand, for example, it must stand alone, and it must support the weight of a book.

Let students explore ways in which the book may be supported by drawing diagrams and discussing their ideas in groups.

After a design has been completed, the book stand can be started.

During the construction stage different designs can be shown and discussed, allowing students the opportunity to use and adapt the ideas of others.

The effectiveness of the design is tested using a recipe book. It is at this stage that modifications and changes may be necessary.

RECORDING AND REPORTING

Testing is an important part of this activity so it is important that students reflect on and record any modifications and changes that they may have made in order to make their model successful.

A good way of doing this is for students to label the parts on their original design that needed modification.

Each student can report orally to the class on the way the stand was constructed, the materials used, design features and its effectiveness in solving the original problem.

FURTHER INVESTIGATIONS

If the original design was effective, students can make the model using other materials, such as wood or plastic.

Investigate ways of folding cardboard to make a stand that does not require the use of tape or glue.

Make up a questionnaire: how big should the stand be, where will it be placed and how it is to be stored?

Use a familiar recipe and adapt one or more ingredients to make something new, and give it a new name. Sample the product in class.

Did you know?

The first breads were made from crushed grains mixed with water to create dough, and cooked on a hot stone or beneath ashes. It was a very coarse, tough, flat bread.

Carry Bag

Students will investigate the strength of materials, and design features to make a useful product.

DESIGN BRIEF

Design, make and test a carry bag that will hold at least 500 grams without breaking. The design must include a handle.

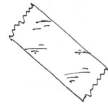

Materials-Resources

- ☐ string
- ☐ twine
- ☐ variety of adhesive tapes
- ☐ cardboard of different thicknesses
- ☐ paper
- ☐ wool
- ☐ fabric scraps
- ☐ old pantihose
- ☐ bamboo
- ☐ stapler
- ☐ glue
- ☐ hole punch

Most paper carry bags, such as supermarket bags, have a reinforced base for strength. Discuss ways in which strength can be given to paper and cardboard, for example, folding—show an example of corrugated cardboard.

Let the students get the feel of 500 grams so that they can compare this to the strength of paper or cardboard.

Discuss with students the areas of the carry bag that might be subject to the most stress, for example, the base and where the handles are attached, and brainstorm possible solutions.

Students should test their carry bag and make any modifications if necessary.

TEACHING POINTS

Before the lesson collect a variety of bags constructed in different ways.

Discuss the purpose and functions of a carry bag.

Discuss features common to carry bags—some form of handle, compartments.

Discuss the types of materials used for carry bags, and ask students which of them are environmentally friendly.

RECORDING AND REPORTING

Before students begin making the bag, a design should be sketched on paper.

After testing, students should make a sketch of the final tested design—labelling the features and indicating where the stress points are.

Have class share time on the success of the carry bags, and tips on improvements. Allow time for students to show and discuss the carry bags they have made.

FURTHER INVESTIGATIONS

Find out the maximum weight the bag is able to carry.

Design a cloth shopping bag. Make the bag using a sewing machine. Make a pattern for others to follow.

Design a partitioned carry bag that can carry a variety of items.

Find out how to make a string bag.

Research methods of carrying items in different countries, for example, in an African village.

Use brochures and catalogues to write shopping lists.

Did you know?

In Egypt, during the eleventh and twelfth centuries, vegetables and spices were carried in paper made from the cloth in which mummies were wrapped. In the 1860s manufacturers in the USA imported shiploads of Egyptian mummies and used the linen wrappings to make brown paper.

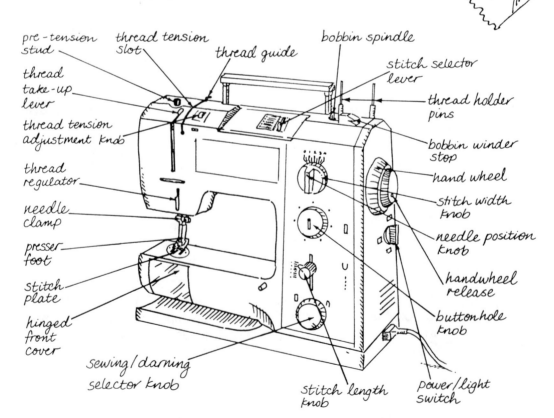

pre-tension stud
thread tension slot
thread guide
bobbin spindle
thread take-up lever
stitch selector lever
thread tension adjustment knob
thread holder pins
thread regulator
bobbin winder stop
needle clamp
hand wheel
presser foot
stitch width knob
stitch plate
needle position knob
hinged front cover
handwheel release
sewing/darning selector knob
buttonhole knob
stitch length knob
power/light switch

Energy Source

Spring in a Box

Students will investigate stored energy and will apply this knowledge to produce a toy using a spring.

DESIGN BRIEF

Make a 'spring in a box' toy.
The box must include a device to
keep the lid closed when not in use.

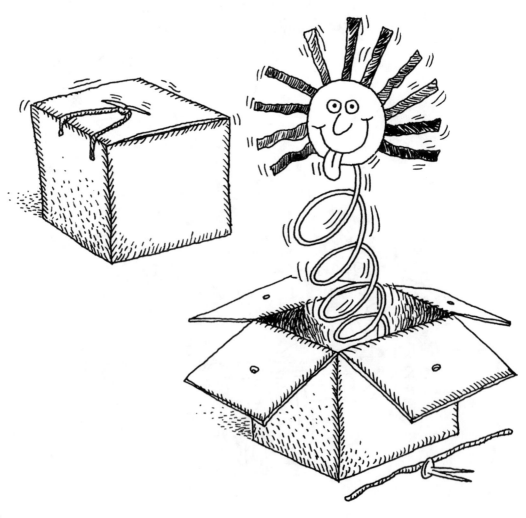

Materials-Resources

- ☐ cardboard
- ☐ paper of different thicknesses
- ☐ different gauged wire
- ☐ split pins
- ☐ pins
- ☐ string
- ☐ adhesive tapes
- ☐ glue
- ☐ art materials
- ☐ ruler
- ☐ template or pattern for box
- ☐ wire springs of different sizes
- ☐ 'Jack-in-the-box' toy (optional)
- ☐ recording sheet (one per student)

Make a box using the pattern provided or get students to rule up a box using their own dimensions.

Ask students how they think a 'Jack-in-the-Box' works. List ideas and discuss, make comparisons with other toys that use stored energy.

Allow students to work and investigate a 'Jack-in-the-Box' (if available).

Demonstrate stored energy by compressing then releasing the spring and observing what happens.

Let students experiment with cardboard and paper strips, using different folding techniques to make springs.

Suggest ways of making wire springs, for example, winding wire around a pencil.

Let students suggest ways of making a closing device, for example, split pin and string.

Students will need to consider the relationship between the length of the paper strip or wire and the length of the finished spring.

Students make up the box (with a closing device), and the spring with a 'head' attached to it (animal, clown, etc.). The spring can be attached to the box with masking tape (suggest to students that this is best done before the box is put together). Some modifications to the spring may be necessary after testing.

75

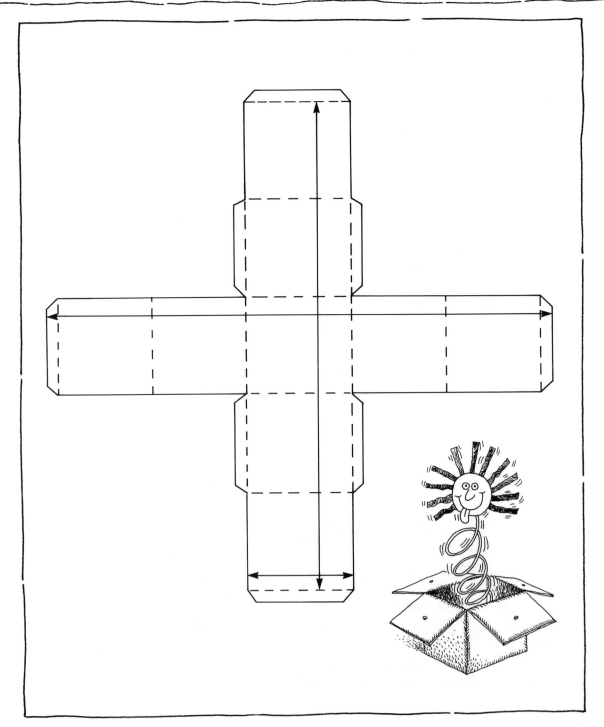

1 Fold strip 1 across strip 2.

strip 1

strip 2

strip 1

strip 2

attached with tape

2 Fold strip 2 up over strip 1.

strip 2

strip 1

3 Fold strip 1 across strip 2.

strip 2

strip 1

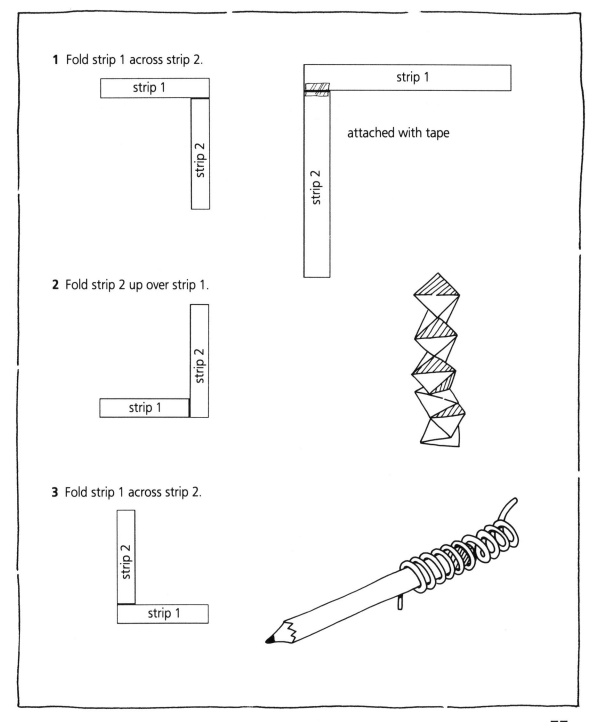

RECORDING AND REPORTING

Students complete a recording sheet.

FURTHER INVESTIGATIONS

Find out how a wind up 'Jack-in-the-Box' works. Present the information as a project using diagrams and labels.

Make a list of the everyday items that use a spring in some way, for example, clocks, pinball machine.

Make a collection of toys powered by stored energy and describe how they work.

Did you know?

A stapler conceals a clever arrangement of springs. It uses a coil spring and a leaf spring to feed the staples along the magazine and then returns the device to its original position.

R Spring in a Box

Name: _____

Materials used	Result

The spring made from

_____

worked the best because

_____

_____

_____

_____

rate
your
design   1   2   3   4   5

Puppets

Students will investigate ways of making joints.

DESIGN BRIEF

Construct an articulated puppet.

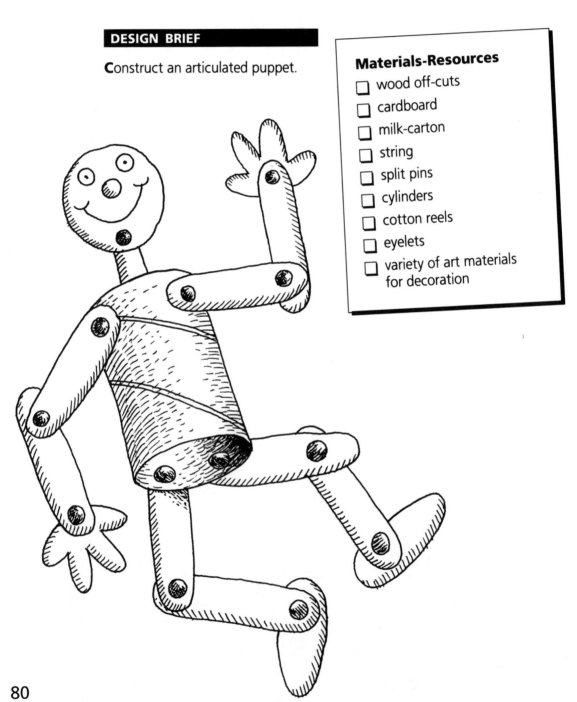

Materials-Resources

- ☐ wood off-cuts
- ☐ cardboard
- ☐ milk-carton
- ☐ string
- ☐ split pins
- ☐ cylinders
- ☐ cotton reels
- ☐ eyelets
- ☐ variety of art materials for decoration

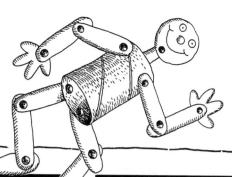

Collect and display books on the history and/or the making of puppets.

Show the students an articulated puppet.

Demonstrate different methods of making joints, for example, cardboard and split pins, cotton reels and string, wood with eyelets.

Students experiment with making joints. This enables students to make an informed choice when selecting the type of puppet to make.

RECORDING AND REPORTING

Students tell the class how their puppet was made and demonstrate how it moves. This can be recorded on videotape, requiring the students to write a script.

The script and the puppet can also be displayed as a static model.

FURTHER INVESTIGATIONS

Create a puppet play using the puppets made by the class, complete with costumes, sets, props, etc.

Make different types of puppets, for example marionette, glove, finger, stick, etc.

Research the history of puppetry and famous puppets such as Punch and Judy.

Investigate shadow puppets and their country of origin.

Arrange for the students to see a professional puppet show.

Produce a puppet play based on a favourite story.

Did you know?

Puppet shows have existed in all civilisations and in almost all periods with written records going back to 500 BC.

The Lighthouse Keeper's Lunch

Students will investigate a pulley system and apply this knowledge to make a model.

DESIGN BRIEF

Make a three-dimensional model of the page-spread shown from *The Lighthouse Keeper's Lunch*. Then make a working model of a pulley system.

Materials-Resources

- ☐ string
- ☐ cotton reels
- ☐ jar lids
- ☐ pulleys
- ☐ cardboard
- ☐ art materials

Pulleys allow loads to be moved with limited strength/effort.

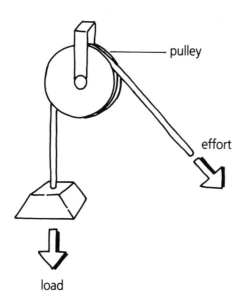

pulley

effort

load

Read *The Lighthouse Keeper's Lunch* and discuss how the lunch is moved from the house to the lighthouse.

Discuss the pulley system used in *The Lighthouse Keeper's Lunch* and let students experiment with making pulleys in small groups. A simple way of demonstrating a pulley is by using a bucket attached to a rope suspended over monkey bars.

The students then use the materials provided to make their own pulleys.

When students are satisfied with their pulley system they can construct the model.

RECORDING AND REPORTING

Display models with labels attached listing the materials used, and a sketch of the pulley system.

FURTHER INVESTIGATIONS

To add an element of surprise, students construct a curtain operated by a pulley system that opens and shuts to expose the model behind it.

Think of and draw a variety of ways of transporting the lunch basket in the story.

Research the history of pulleys.

List everyday uses of pulleys, for example, escalators, lifts, cranes.

Test the strength of the student's pulleys.

Did you know?
Pulleys were used over 3000 years ago.

Batteries & Bulbs— Illuminated Scene

Students will investigate how a simple electric circuit is made and apply this knowledge to produce a model.

DESIGN BRIEF

Design and construct a scene that has a lit globe as part of the model.

Materials-Resources

- ☐ batteries (6 volt are most suitable)
- ☐ wire
- ☐ small globes
- ☐ heavy cardboard
- ☐ art materials (paint, Textas, etc.)
- ☐ circuit sheet (one per student or group)

Using the circuit sheet as a starting point, lead students to discover how to light the globe and form a simple circuit.

After students have experimented in trying to light the globe, discuss the circuit sheet and share ideas about why some examples did not work.

Students, individually or in groups, are now given the opportunity to apply this knowledge in creating a scene that incorporates a globe. It may be necessary to brainstorm a few ideas with students first. Some examples are: beach scene with a lighthouse; Christmas tree with decorations; Rudolph the Red-Nosed Reindeer, a street scene with a street light.

TEACHING POINTS

Ask students what they know about batteries and list this on blackboard or large sheet of paper.

It is important to warn students that batteries contain acid, and if the casing of the battery is damaged the leaking chemicals could be dangerous.

You may wish to demonstrate to students how a simple circuit works using a 6 volt battery, or allow students time to experiment individually or in small groups.

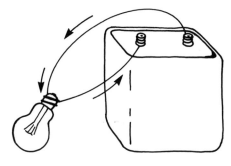

The wire is connected to the '+' and '−' on the top of the battery. The 'circuit' is completed when the electricity goes from battery → bulb →battery.

Suggest simple ways of making background diorama, for example, folding, scoring or hinging cardboard.

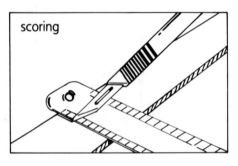

scoring

snapping

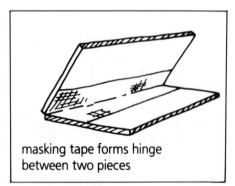

masking tape forms hinge between two pieces

Groups and/or individuals report to the class and demonstrate how their diorama works.

FURTHER INVESTIGATIONS

Students could further develop electric circuits to include simple switching devices.

Research the history of batteries and present as a project.

Test the life of a variety of brands of batteries by using a torch, or battery-operated toy, and record results.

Investigate battery-driven cars.

Did you know?

In 1800, Alessandro Volta published details of the first battery. Volta's battery produced electricity using the chemical reaction between certain solutions and metal electrodes. The electrical unit 'volt' is named after him.

Batteries and Bulbs

R

Circuit Sheet

Name: _____

Colour in the circuit that you think will light the globe.

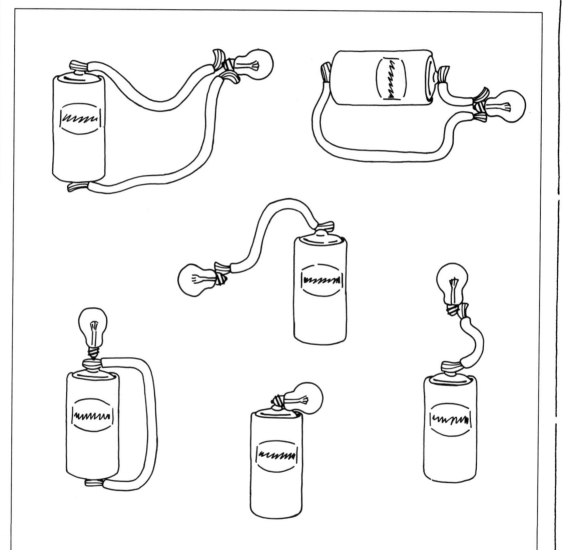

Work with a friend to find out if you were correct.

Use 2 wires, a bulb and a battery.

Try out each one.

© Helen Clayfield, Robyn Hyatt

87

Vehicles

Students will investigate the movement of wheels using an axle, and learn about the complexity of 'real' items by using simple models.

DESIGN BRIEF

Design and construct a vehicle that has moving wheels.

Materials-Resources

- [ ] cardboard
- [ ] cardboard boxes
- [ ] straws
- [ ] skewers
- [ ] balsa-wood
- [ ] plastic wheels (optional)
- [ ] cardboard wheels
- [ ] plastic lids
- [ ] paper plates
- [ ] split pins
- [ ] wire
- [ ] a variety of adhesive tapes
- [ ] glue
- [ ] milk-cartons
- [ ] juice bottles
- [ ] toy car or truck that has a visible axle
- [ ] single hole punch
- [ ] large beads

TEACHING POINTS

Discuss with students how they think wheels are attached to the body of a vehicle. Using a milk-carton and cardboard wheels, demonstrate student responses, for example, stick wheels flat to the side of the carton with masking tape, ask students if the wheels can turn.

Show students the axle on the bottom of the toy car or truck.

Demonstrate using cardboard wheels and straws, how the wheels can work in pairs to assist the vehicle to move. Discuss ways of ensuring that the wheels stay on the axle, for example, tape wound around the axle, beads, small circle of cardboard or balsa-wood, etc.

Students design their model on paper then select their materials.

When completed, the model is tested by being rolled down a slightly-inclined surface.

Students observe how the wheels rotate and make modifications to their model if required.

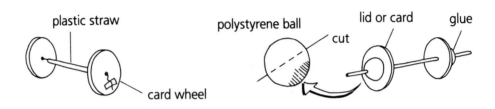

plastic straw

card wheel

polystyrene ball

cut

lid or card   glue

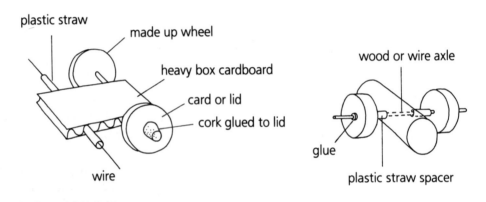

plastic straw

made up wheel

heavy box cardboard

card or lid

cork glued to lid

wire

wood or wire axle

glue

plastic straw spacer

RECORDING AND REPORTING

Students' original designs are displayed with the models and a report discussing the effectiveness of the wheels and axles.

FURTHER INVESTIGATIONS

Using the same design, construct a model using different materials.

Investigate how rubber tyres are made and present the findings in pictorial form.

Find out how a water-wheel works and what it is used for.

Investigate vehicles that have more than four wheels.

Did you know?

Rubber tyres are reinforced by a network of nylon, rayon or steel cords and webbing. Most cars today use radial-ply tyres with cords running radially out from the wheel's centre.

Bridge

Students will investigate the variations of design and structure needed to cope with different situations.

Construct a bridge that will span the 'river' and support the weight of three model cars. The bridge may only have one support in the river.

Materials-Resources

- [ ] photographs or pictures of different types of bridges made from different materials (if possible)
- [ ] blue crepe paper or cellophane
- [ ] cardboard
- [ ] balsa-wood
- [ ] straws
- [ ] icy-pole sticks
- [ ] cardboard tubes
- [ ] adhesive tape
- [ ] glue
- [ ] split pins
- [ ] boxes
- [ ] Matchbox cars or similar
- [ ] Lego Technic (optional)
- [ ] camera (optional)

TEACHING POINTS

Before you begin, show students the photographs of the bridges. Discuss the similarities and differences between them. Use terms such as span, support, arch and structure.

Students may notice that some bridges have crossed beams in their design. Take the opportunity to demonstrate 'rigidity' with the students.

If using Lego Technic, make and demonstrate how the shape can be moved, add a cross piece. What happens to the structure? If Lego is unavailable, cardboard strips and split pins will work to demonstrate the principle.

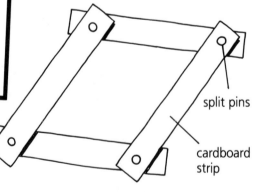

split pins

cardboard strip

With this model the strips can be moved in all directions.

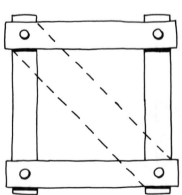

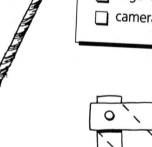

Add a cross piece and the model become rigid.

Unroll the crepe paper for a few metres along the classroom floor. This paper becomes the river. If paper is unavailable mark the river in chalk.

Students may work individually, however this is an excellent activity for co-operative group work.

As students are working, discuss the differences, if any, between their design and model. Why was the design modified?

Test the bridges, do they satisfy the requirements of the design brief?

RECORDING AND REPORTING

Groups or individuals sketch their design before construction begins.

A good way of recording the students' efforts is to photograph each model. Place the photographs in an album together with students' descriptions on how successful the bridge was, materials used, techniques used to provide strength and support etc. and the original design.

FURTHER INVESTIGATIONS

Investigate some famous bridges from around the world, and present as a project.

Research stories, poems, rhymes and songs about bridges.

Find out about the ways people and goods are transported across stretches of water without the aid of a bridge.

Did you know?

Australia's oldest bridge is in Richmond, Tasmania. Spanning the waters of the Coal River, it was built by convicts between 1823 and 1825. Legend has it that the ghost of an overseer who was murdered by the convicts still haunts the bridge.

Stored Energy Boat

Students will investigate stored energy and use this knowledge to construct a model.

DESIGN BRIEF

Design and make a boat that moves as a result of stored energy and test its effectiveness in water.

Materials-Resources

- [ ] thick cardboard
- [ ] balsa-wood
- [ ] milk-cartons
- [ ] 2-litre plastic juice bottles
- [ ] rubber bands of different sizes
- [ ] a variety of adhesive tapes
- [ ] large water trough, sink or baby's bath

TEACHING POINTS

Before you begin, prepare a model to demonstrate stored energy.

Ask students to predict what will happen when you release the model, and why. Would the result be the same if you used string instead of rubber bands? If not, explain why.

List all the things that work by using stored energy, such as wind-up toys and solar-powered lights.

Discuss how stored energy could power a model boat using the same principle as the demonstration.

A

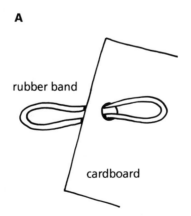

rubber band

cardboard

B

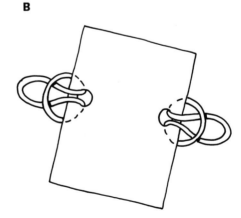

twist cardboard — release to show stored energy

95

Students design their own boat using the materials available.

It may be helpful to provide a simple design for a stored energy boat to allow some students a starting point.

Students need to consider the materials they will use in their boat, remembering that their model will be tested in water.

Students sketch a design before they begin to make their boat.

After testing the boat and making any necessary modifications, students list step by step instructions, that can be easily understood by others, on how to make the boat.

FURTHER INVESTIGATIONS

Design and make a more complex model using other materials such as plywood and non water-soluble adhesives.

Design and make a toy that uses stored energy for movement.

Investigate how paddle-steamers work and make a model.

Research paddle-steamers in Australia's early days of river transport.

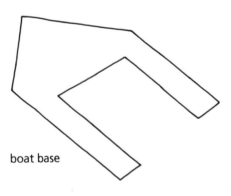

boat base

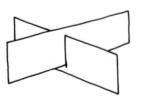

propeller made from joined cardboard

Did you know?

River boats were a vital link between the inland and coastal parts of Victoria in the late 1800s. Mildura was one of the busiest inland ports and often five paddle-steamers at a time would be berthed at the wharf.

Glossary

articulated   jointed object

axle   rod connecting wheels

battery casing   outside covering of a battery

cantilever   construction technique using a beam or girder fixed at one end only

circuit   path of electrical current

concept maps   method of grouping brainstorm ideas

coping saw   U-shaped saw used for intricate cutting

facade   outward appearance of building

flange   method of joining by cutting and bending

marionette   puppet controlled by string

perspex   light, transparent plastic

pinking shears   scissors with serrated cutting edge

pole house   house constructed on poles to allow for ventilation

pulley   device used to lift an object by using a downward force

recording sheet   written/illustrated record of design brief

scoring   marking the surface of a material with a sharp implement before folding or cutting

stored energy   energy stored within an object ready for release

team-teaching   two or more teachers planning and working together

template   guide/pattern used to trace around or to mark drill/nail holes

tenon-saw   small, strong saw used for fine work

wattle and daub   method of building construction using a framework of twigs and branches covered with plaster

DATE DUE

MAY 1 6 '0?			
JUN 1 3 2006			
JUL 05 2006			

GAYLORD

PRINTED IN U.S.A.